# the source

## arrangements for worship groups

### book 3

**C instruments**

**arranged by Chris Mitchell**

Kevin Mayhew

We hope you enjoy the music in this book.
Further copies of this and the other books in the series are available
from your local music shop or Christian bookshop.

In case of difficulty, please contact the publisher direct:

The Sales Department
KEVIN MAYHEW LTD
Rattlesden
Bury St Edmunds
Suffolk IP30 0SZ

Phone 01449 737978
Fax 01449 737834
E-mail info@kevinmayhewltd.com

Please ask for our complete catalogue of outstanding Church Music.

First published in Great Britain in 1998 by Kevin Mayhew Ltd.

© Copyright 1998 Kevin Mayhew Ltd.

ISBN 1 84003 124 7
ISMN M 57004 207 4
Catalogue No: 1470303

0 1 2 3 4 5 6 7 8 9

Cover designed by Jaquetta Sergeant.

Music arrangements by Chris Mitchell
Music Editor: Donald Thomson
Music setting by Chris Mitchell and Vernon Turner

Printed and bound in Great Britain

**the source** will be developed into a major resource for the churches. It is already available in the following editions

| | | |
|---|---|---|
| Words Only | ISBN | 1 84003 121 2 |
| | Catalogue No. | 1470101 |
| | | |
| Full Music | ISBN | 1 84003 120 4 |
| | ISMN | M 57004 204 3 |
| | Catalogue No. | 1470104 |
| | | |
| Complete Acetate Masters | ISBN | 1 84003 119 0 |
| | Catalogue No. | 1470201 |

Arrangements for Worship Groups:

| | | |
|---|---|---|
| Book 1 for C instruments | ISBN | 1 84003 122 0 |
| | ISMN | M 57004 205 0 |
| | Catalogue No. | 1470301 |
| | | |
| Book 1 for B♭ instruments | ISBN | 1 84003 128 X |
| | ISMN | M 57004 211 1 |
| | Catalogue No. | 1470307 |
| | | |
| Book 2 for C instruments | ISBN | 1 84003 123 9 |
| | ISMN | M 57004 206 7 |
| | Catalogue No. | 1470302 |
| | | |
| Book 2 for B♭ instruments | ISBN | 1 84003 129 8 |
| | ISMN | M 57004 212 8 |
| | Catalogue No. | 1470308 |
| | | |
| Book 3 for C instruments | ISBN | 1 84003 124 7 |
| | ISMN | M 57004 207 4 |
| | Catalogue No. | 1470303 |
| | | |
| Book 3 for B♭ instruments | ISBN | 1 84003 130 1 |
| | ISMN | M 57004 213 5 |
| | Catalogue No. | 1470309 |

# 201  I cry out for your hand
*(Good to me)*

Craig Musseau

## 202 If you are encouraged

Graham Kendrick

2 verses

## 203 I give you all the honour
### (I worship you)

Carl Tuttle

3 verses

**Majestically**

## 204  I have come to love you

Matt Redman

3 verses

## 205  I have made you too small
### (Be magnified)

Lynn DeShazo

2 verses

## 206  I heard the voice of Jesus say (Tune 1)

Traditional English Melody

3 verses

## 206a  I heard the voice of Jesus say (Tune 2)

John Bacchus Dykes

3 verses

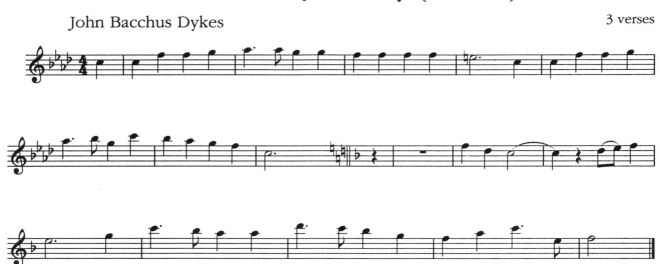

# 207 I just want to be where you are

Don Moen

# 208  I just want to praise you

Arthur Tannous

# 209  I know a place
## *(At the cross)*

Randy and Terry Butler

# 210 I know it

Darlene Zschech

## 211 I lift my eyes up to the mountains
### *(Psalm 121)*
Brian Doerksen

## 212 I lift my hands
### *(I will serve no foreign god)*
Andre Kempen

## 213 I love to be in your presence
Paul Baloche and Ed Kerr

## 214 I love you, Lord, and I lift my voice

Laurie Klein

## 215 I love you, Lord
### *(Holy is your name)*
Mike Day and Dave Bell

## 216 I love your presence

Fabienne Pons

## 217 I'm accepted, I'm forgiven

Rob Hayward

## 218 I'm gonna click

Capt. Alan J. Price

4 verses

## 219 Immanuel, O Immanuel

Graham Kendrick

**Worshipfully, but with strength**

# 220 Immortal, invisible, God only wise

Traditional Welsh hymn melody

5 verses

# 221 I'm so secure
## (In your hands)

Reuben Morgan

2 verses

## 222 I'm special

Graham Kendrick

**With feeling**

## 223 I'm standing here to testify
### *(Come to the light)*

Kevin Prosch

2 verses

**With a steady rhythm**

## 224 I'm your child

Richard Hubbard

3 verses

## 225 In Christ alone

Shawn Craig and Don Koch

## 226 I need you more

Lindell Cooley and Bruce Haynes

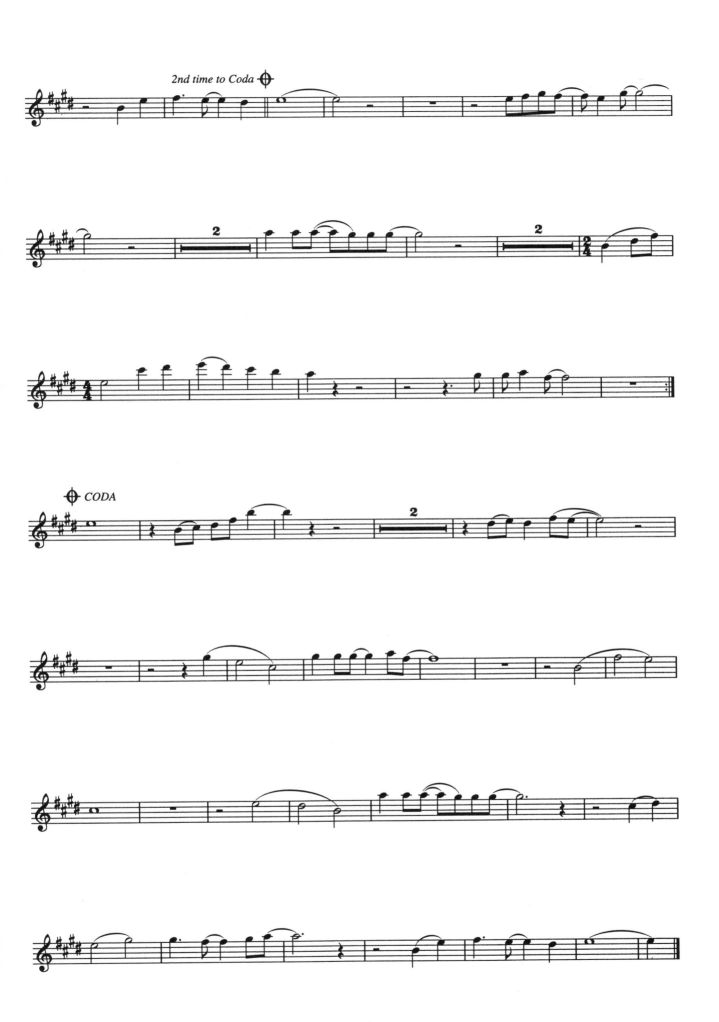

2nd time to Coda

CODA

21

# 227 In every circumstance

David Fellingham

**With a 12/8 feel**

## 228 In heavenly armour
*(The battle belongs to the Lord)*

Jamie Owens-Collins

3 verses

**With strength**

*Verse*

*Chorus*

*last time*

## 229 In moments like these

David Graham

*to repeat*     *last time*

## 230 In my life, Lord
### (Lord, be glorified)
Bob Kilpatrick

2 verses

**Prayerfully**

to repeat | last time

## 231 In the morning when I rise
### (All I want)
Andy Park

3 verses

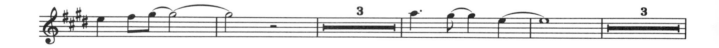

to verse 2

Fine

to middle section

## 232 In the presence of a holy God

Mark Altrogge

2 verses

## 233 In the secret

Andy Park

2 verses

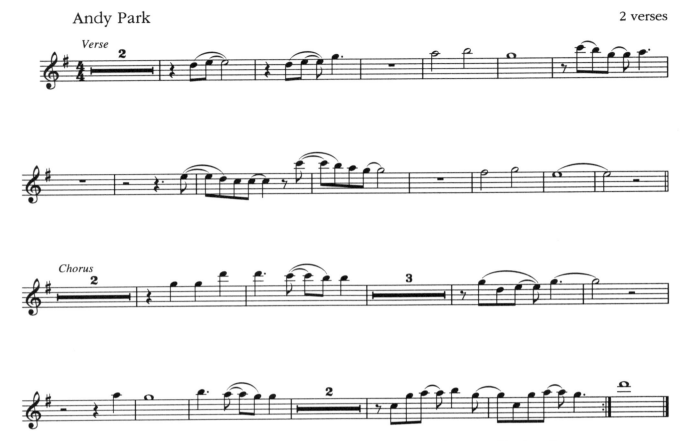

## 234 In the tomb so cold
### *(Christ is risen!)*

Graham Kendrick

4 verses

**Triumphantly**

## 235 I reach up high

Judy Bailey

2 verses

## 236 I receive your love

2 verses

Paul Armstrong

## 237 Is anyone thirsty?

Graham Kendrick

## 238 I see the Lord

Chris Falson

## 239  I sing a simple song of love
*(Arms of love)*

Craig Musseau

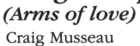

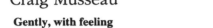

## 240  I sing praises

Terry MacAlmon

2 verses

## 241  Is it true today
### (History maker)

Martin Smith

## 242 Isn't he beautiful

John Wimber

2 verses

# 243 I stand amazed in the presence

Charles H. Gabriel

5 verses

# 244 I stand before the presence

Mavis Ford

# 245  I stand before your throne

Matthew Ling

2 verses

## 246  I, the Lord of sea and sky
### *(Here I am, Lord)*
Dan Schutte

3 verses

## 247  It is to you
Duke Kerr

## 248 It's our confession, Lord
*(Sweet mercies)*

David Ruis

# 249 It's rising up

Matt Redman and Martin Smith

3 verses

# 250 It's your blood

Michael Christ

## 251 I've found a friend

*(Joy in the Holy Ghost)*

Russell Fragar

2 verses

## 252 I've got a love song

Matt Redman

5 verses

## 253 I walk by faith

Chris Falson

## 254 I want to be a tree that's bearing fruit
### (I want to be a blooming tree)

Doug Horley

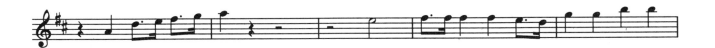

to repeat

last time

3

## 255 I want to be out of my depth in your love

Doug Horley and Noel Richards

Gently

1.  2.  Fine

1.  2.  D.S. al Fine

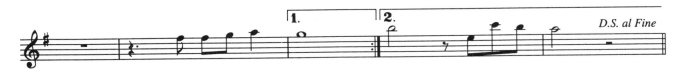

## 256 I want to serve the purpose of God
### *(In my generation)*
Mark Altrogge

4 verses

## 257 I went to the enemy's camp
### *(Enemy's camp)*
Richard Black

## 258  I will be yours
*(Eternity)*

Brian Doerksen

## 259  I will build my church

Graham Kendrick

# 260 I will change your name

D.J. Butler

Tenderly

# 261 I will dance, I will sing
## (Undignified)

Matt Redman

With life and energy

## 262 I will enter his gates
### *(He has made me glad)*
Leona von Brethorst

With pace and swing

## 263 I will lift my voice

Geoff Bullock

2 verses

## 264 I will never be the same again

Geoff Bullock

## 265 I will offer up my life
### *(This thankful heart)*

Matt Redman

2 verses

Gently

## 266 I will praise you all my life
*(O faithful God)*

Mark Altrogge

## 267  I will seek you

Matthew Lockwood

## 268  I will seek your face, O Lord

Noel and Tricia Richards

2 verses

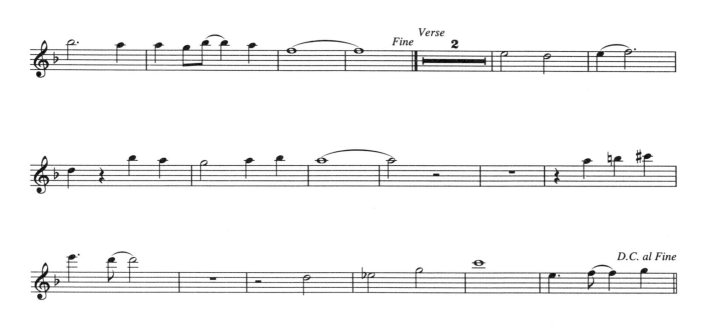

## 269 I will wave my hands

Ian Smale

## 270 I will worship
### *(You alone are worthy of my praise)*

David Ruis

2 verses

**Worshipfully, with strength**

## 271 I worship you, Almighty God

Sondra Corbett

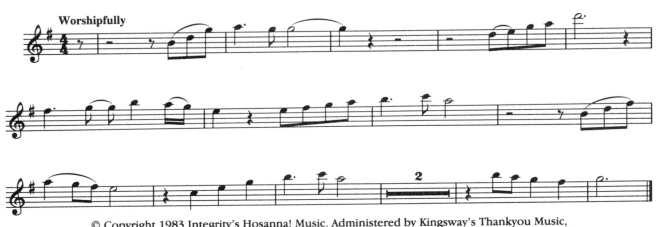

## 272 I worship you, O Lamb of God

2 verses

Graham Kendrick

## 273 Jesus, at your name
### *(You are the Christ)*
Chris Bowater

## 274 Jesus Christ
### *(Once again)*
Matt Redman

2 verses

**Thoughtfully, not too fast**

## 275 Jesus Christ is Lord of all
*(Jesus is our battle cry)*

Graham Kendrick

## 276 Jesus Christ is risen today

from *Lyra Davidica*

## 277 Jesus Christ is the Lord of all

Steve Israel and Gerrit Gustafson

# 278 Jesus, God's righteousness revealed
## *(This kingdom)*
Geoff Bullock

2 verses

## 279 Jesus, how lovely you are

Dave Bolton

4 verses

**Worshipfully**
*Chorus*

## 280 Jesus! I am resting, resting

James Mountain

4 verses

# 281 Jesus, I am thirsty
## (More of you)
Don Harris and Martin J. Nystrom

# 282 Jesus is greater

Gill Hutchinson

## 283 Jesus is King

Wendy Churchill

4 verses

## 284 Jesus is Lord!

David Mansell

3 verses

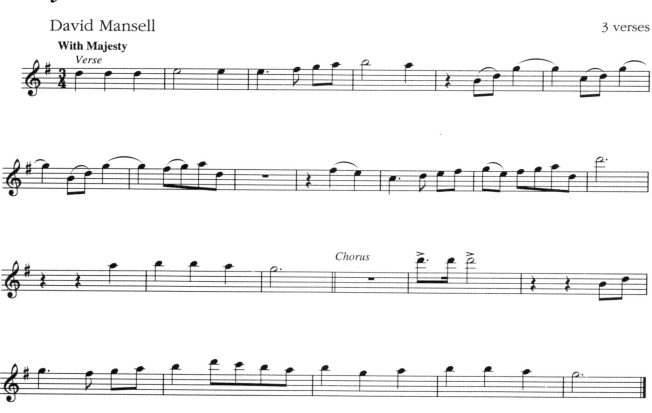

# 285 Jesus is the name we honour

*(Jesus is our God)*

Philip Lawson Johnston

3 verses

## 286 Jesus, Jesus
### *(Holy and anointed one)*
John Barnett

With feeling

1st and last times / 2nd time
Fine

D.C. al Fine

## 287 Jesus, Jesus, Jesus

Chris Bowater

Worshipfully

# 288 Jesus, Jesus, you have the name
### *(Hearts on fire)*
David Hadden

# 289 Jesus' love has got under our skin
## *(Under our skin)*
Graham Kendrick

3 verses

# 290 Jesus, lover of my soul

John Ezzy, Daniel Grul and Stephen McPherson

# 291 Jesus, name above all names

Nadia Hearn

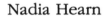

## 292 Jesus put this song into our hearts

Graham Kendrick

**'Hebrew' style, getting faster**
*(verse 5 instrumental)*

5 verses

## 293 Jesus reigns

Colin Owen

3 verses

# 294 Jesus, remember me

Jacques Berthier

# 295 Jesus, restore to us again

Graham Kendrick

5 verses

## 296 Jesus shall take the highest honour

Chris Bowater

## 297 Jesus, take me as I am

Dave Bryant

# 298 Jesus, the name high over all

Thomas Phillips

6 verses

# 299 Jesus, we celebrate your victory

John Gibson

2 verses

# 300 Jesus, we enthrone you

Paul Kyle